Ana Valéria Borges de Carvalho Melo
André L F C Melo

The Motor Development Scale by Rosa Neto (2002), a review

Ana Valéria Borges de Carvalho Melo
André L F C Melo

The Motor Development Scale by Rosa Neto (2002), a review

Human Psychomotricity Studies

ScienciaScripts

Imprint

Cover image: www.ingimage.com

This book is a translation from the original published under ISBN 978-620-2-40573-7.

Publisher:
Sciencia Scripts
is a trademark of
Dodo Books Indian Ocean Ltd. and OmniScriptum S.R.L publishing group

120 High Road, East Finchley, London, N2 9ED, United Kingdom
Str. Armeneasca 28/1, office 1, Chisinau MD-2012, Republic of Moldova, Europe
Printed at: see last page
ISBN: 978-620-8-31628-0

ACKNOWLEDGMENTS

This unique moment in my career has only been possible thanks to the sum of all the people who have shared moments of my life and every minute of my journey. Over the last few years, I've learned that it's the relationships I've established that make me who I am: a being in the process of transformation.

I thank God for showering me with blessings, and I also take this opportunity to ask him to allow me to become a better person every day, helping to develop my profession and, above all, helping people whenever possible in my life.

To my parents, Valderi and Evaneide, who became channels for the expression of divine love, taking care of my life from its earliest days. For all their love and dedication.

To my fiancé, Andre Luiz, with whom I share my journey through life, who teaches me so much about love, care, affection, tenderness, help and who has made my dreams his own.

To my friends, so many and so different, sources of delight and joy, who share with me the challenge and pleasure of living. Especially Daisy

Oliveira, for her help and companionship during these five and a half years of academic life.

Sometimes we feel that what we do is just a drop in the ocean. But the sea would be smaller if it lacked one drop.

(Mother Teresa of Calcutta)

SUMMARY

This research seeks to discover in current literature the importance of Rosa Neto's Motor Development Scale (2002) as an instrument for assessing children's motor development. To this end, the following objective was established: To ascertain the contributions of Rosa Neto's Motor Development Scale (2002) as an instrument for assessing children's motor development. This is done by relating motor development and psychomotricity, presenting the Rosa Neto motor development scale as an instrument for assessing motor development and studying the importance given to the Rosa Neto motor development scale by the scientific community. This is a bibliographical study. After a theoretical review of the data, three basic themes were established for discussion: the relationship between motor development and psychomotricity, the importance of motor development in the learning process and the importance of the Rosa Neto Motor Development Scale in the study and research of psychomotricity. The results were as follows: Rosa Neto (2002) has made a major contribution to studies into motor development, because with the creation of his scale, a capable and insightful instrument for measuring the development of motor skills emerged in the scientific world. For the scientific community, this instrument conveys a high degree of reliability for the analysis of motor development, while it is a highly accessible and easy-to-use mechanism for carrying out tests, which makes it possible to investigate this process to a greater extent.

Keywords: Psychomotricity, motor development, Learning, Rosa Neto Motor Development Scale.

SUMMARY

1. INTRODUCTION

It is well known in the scientific community that there has been an increase in studies on motor development. One of the reasons for the growing interest in motor development is the relationship between motor development and cognitive development, since there is a close relationship between what a child is capable of learning (cognitive development) and what they are capable of doing (motor development).

O motor development is a continuous and lasting process that takes place throughout a person's life. However, the acquisition of a broad mastery of motor skills is characterized by childhood, as this enables the development of the body in postures, both static and dynamic, moving through the environment, whether walking, running, jumping or manipulating objects through throwing, receiving, kicking, writing, etc. Although people are different from one another, the sequences of their motor development are the most reliable and effective because of the changes that occur in the body over time.

Psychomotricity is very important for the human being because it is a process in which various changes occur in an individual's development (cognitive, social and cultural), acquiring a greater ability to perform and control certain movements with facilities built up over time.

However, psychomotor development is characterized by a maturation that integrates both movement, rhythm and spatial construction, as well as knowledge of objects, positions, body schema and, finally, words.

According to Nunez and Berruezzo (1994) Psychomotricity is about linking the apparently disconnected elements of the same evolution: psychic development and motor development.

In order for these skills to be developed, children need to be given opportunities to perform them. O movement is of great importance, because it is through the execution of movements that people interact with the environment, relate to others, learn about themselves, their limits, abilities and solve problems.

School Physical Education, according to Perez, Boeck and Campos (2000), is an integral part of the Educational System and must use the knowledge of Psychomotor Education to provide the overall development of the child. It also provides a structured and appropriate environment for the child, helping to promote human development.

O motor development is a sequential process, related to chronological age, brought about by the interaction between task requirements, the individual's biology and environmental conditions, and is inherent to social, intellectual and emotional changes. O human being, from conception to old age, undergoes various transformations. Every human organism has a biological logic, an organization, a mature and evolutionary timetable, a door open to interaction and stimulation. Between birth and adulthood, profound changes take place. The child's motor possibilities evolve greatly with age and become increasingly varied, complete and complex.

It's also important to point out that the acquisition of motor skills is closely linked to the development of spatial-temporal perception of the body, and these skills constitute basic mastery components for both motor learning and school education activities. According to Rosa Neto et all (2010), this means that by achieving good motor control, children are building the basic notions for their intellectual development.

From this perspective, it is understood that it is necessary to develop and study motor development assessment tools that make it possible to ascertain and intuit the motor stages of children and young people.

There are countless tests and scales for assessing a child's motor development, however, according to Rosa Neto et all (2010), almost none of these instruments can completely cover all aspects of development.

However, one of the scales that tends to contribute to a complete and enlightening assessment of motor development is Rosa Neto's Motor Development Scale (MDS), as it has a method of applying tests that are attractive to changes, comprising a set of diversified tests of graduated difficulty, covering different areas of motor development.

This research seeks to find answers to the following question in the current literature: What is the importance of Rosa Neto's Motor Development Scale as an instrument for assessing children's motor development?

In view of the above, the general aim of this study was to investigate the contributions of Rosa Neto's Motor Development Scale as a tool for assessing children's motor development. Relating motor development and psychomotricity, presenting Rosa Neto's Motor Development Scale as an instrument for assessing motor development and checking the importance given to Rosa Neto's MDE by the scientific community.

What was realized from the study was that the Motor Development Scale proposed by Rosa Neto was presented to the scientific community as an excellent instrument for checking the development of motor skills in children and young people.

2. PSYCHOMOTRICITY: HISTORY AND CONCEPTS

The word psychomotricity has its origins in the Greek word "psyche" which means "soul" and the Latin verb "moto" which means to move. In other words, psychomotricity means "the soul of moving".

The Brazilian Society of Psychomotricity (2003) defines psychomotricity as the science that studies man through his body in movement and in relation to his internal and external world. It is related to the process of maturation, where the body is the origin of cognitive, affective and organic acquisitions. It is underpinned by three basic skills: o movement, o intellect and o affect.

Psychomotricity is defined by Fonseca (2002, p.15) as "an object of study that encompasses the relationships between neurocerebral organization, cognitive organization and the expressive organization of action", in other words, it comprises action, with execution and elaboration not being dissociated.

We thus understand that psychomotricity admits that the individual is integrated into their body, is a junction of the physical, social and affective, is in constant transformation, modifying and being modified by the environment.

According to Lima and Barbosa (2011) psychomotricity is nothing more than relating through the breath, соmo a means of becoming aware that unites o being body, o being mind, o being spirit, o being nature and o being society. Psychomotricity is therefore associated with affectivity and personality, because the individual uses their body to show how they feel.

According to Lima and Barbosa (2011), psychomotor development is extremely important in preventing problems related to learning and in re-educating tone, posture, directionality, laterality and rhythm.

In the evolutionary process of psychomotricity, American and European civilization have been the most striking, with the French school standing out, which has had an incisive influence on the direction psychomotricity has taken (BUENO, 1998).

It was in France at the end of the 19th century and the beginning of the 20th century that the term psychomotricity originated. It was initially studied in conjunction with child neuropsychiatry. The studies dealt with the motor weakness syndrome and the mental weakness syndrome. This was the first time that the term Psychomotricity was used to refer to children (SILVA E FALKENBACK, 2006).

However, it was Dupre who first mentioned the term psychomotricity in 1920, meaning an intertwining of thought and movement. He observed the existence of a close relationship between psychological abnormalities and motor abnormalities, which led him to formulate the term (OLIVEIRA, 2001).

Henry Wallon (1879-1962), a doctor, psychologist and pedagogue, is probably the great pioneer of psychomotricity as a scientific field. According to Fonseca (1995), Wallon provided definitive observations on the neurological development of the newborn and the psychomotor development of the child. Wallon says that "movement is the only expression and the first instrument of the psyche". O movement, which is action, o thought and language are inseparable units. O movement and o thought in act, and o thought and o movement without act. From his work it was possible to build, by synthesizing many currents and theories, a new therapeutic technique, the aim of which was the re-education of motor functions.

The doctor Edouard Guilmain began psychomotor practice in 1935 with a method called psychomotor re-education, which consisted of applying batteries of psychomotor tests to assess the child's profile. A standard psychomotor examination and a program of sessions are established according to the characteristics of the individual's motor disorders, guiding the therapist's intervention modalities (SILVA and FALKENBACK, 2006).

According to this development, at the beginning of the 20th century, the notion of psychomotricity focused on the child's psychomotor development. Then the relationship between delayed motor development and intellectual delay was studied, which was called "psychomotor parallelism". This was followed by studies into the development of manual dexterity and motor skills as a function of age, until the current position of Psychomotricity was reached, which is to overcome motor problems and work on the relationship between gesture, affectivity and the quality of communication through them (BUENO, 1998, p.123).

Piaget (1896-1980) also played an important role in the study of psychomotricity. He studied the interrelationships between psychomotricity and perception through extensive experimentation. He describes the importance of the sensorimotor period and motor skills, especially before the acquisition of language, in the development of intelligence. Mental development is built up gradually. It is a progressive balance, a continuous passage from a state of lower balance to a state of higher balance. Intelligence, therefore, is an adaptation to the environment. For this to happen, it is necessary, initially, to manipulate the objects in the environment with the modification of primary reflexes (OLIVEIRA, 2002).

In the 1970s, due to the influence of Wallen's work, work on psychomotor education emerged by Le Boulch, who, since 1966, in his book "Education through Movement", had the initial objective of sensitizing primary school teachers to the problem of psychomotor education at school, since it was a context unfavorable to the pedagogy of the time, centered on the acquisition of "Basic School Skills". Added to this was the work of L. Pick, P. Vayer, Andre Lapierre, Bernard Auconturier, Defontaine, J. C. Coste and others who saw psychomotor education at this time as an original way of helping maladjusted children to develop their potential and gain access to the world of school. The authors brought knowledge and solutions inspired by genetic psychology, which shows that children develop knowledge of themselves and the world around them through their actions. With these new contributions, psychomotricity differentiated itself from other disciplines, acquiring its own specificity and autonomy (LEVIN, 2000).

Levin (2000) states that psychoanalytic contributions became part of the theoretical and methodological interests of psychomotricity, and in 1977, Sami Ali proposed a link between psychoanalytic theories and psychomotricity. Psychomotricity thus incorporates psychoanalytic concepts such as the unconscious, transference, body image, sublimation and others into its theoretical constructions, forming an outline of a psychoanalytic theory of psychomotricity.

As a result, we realize that although there are many different conceptualizations of what psychomotricity is, it is a theoretical construct that has undergone changes throughout history and by scholars on the subject. However, it can be defined as the realization of thought through a cohesive, precise and harmonious motor act.

3. MOTOR DEVELOPMENT AND BASIC ELEMENTS OF MOTOR SKILLS

The study and definition of motor development is a highly debated topic, discussed mainly in the early childhood education period by various authors, including those from the field of psychology. In order to define motor development, this study presents the views of various authors and scholars on the subject.

In childhood, motor development is characterized by the acquisition of a wide range of motor skills, which enables children to master their bodies in different postures, to move around the environment in different ways and also to handle objects in different ways (SANTOS et. al, 2004).

Oliveira (2001) states that the entire basic sequence of motor development is based on the developmental sequence of the brain, since the progressive change in an individual's motor capacity is triggered by their interaction with their environment and the task they are engaged in. In other words, a person's hereditary characteristics, combined with specific environmental conditions and the very requirements of the task the individual performs, determine the amount and extent of motor skill acquisition and aptitude improvement.

Motor functions are described as basic by Fonseca (1995) as spatial-temporal organization, fine and broad coordination, body tone, balance, laterality and others. Deficiency in any of these elements can lead to a series of maladjustments in cognitive, physical, emotional and social functions.

According to Rosa Neto (2002), fine motor skills are a set of activities involving the movement of segments of the human body in synchrony with vision in order to obtain a precise response to a task.

Velasco (1994) states that fine motor coordination involves small muscles and the ability to manipulate small objects with precise movements, which requires a certain amount of neurological maturation. Children "see" with their fingers.

Lopes & Farjalla (2009) state that through fine motor skills, a large number of smaller muscles are controlled, which are responsible for the precision of movements, providing a strong stimulus for the maturation of the central nervous system, which is still in the growth phase.

According to Velasco (1994), a child who does not yet know and recognize his own self and possibilities does not coordinate his movements in time and space.

Lopes & Farjalla (2009) consider global motricity to be the combination of movements that allows the action of various muscle groups to be combined in a sequence of movements with maximum efficiency, economy and speed, when speed and strength are involved.

Global Motricity is defined by Rosa Neto (2002) as the child's ability to make gestures, attitudes, movements and rhythms, sometimes allowing us to get to know and understand them better rather than seeking information about them in the words they say.

Rosa Neto (2002) believes that balance is the primordial basis of all the differentiated actions of the body segments, as imbalance results in bodily, mental and spiritual fatigue, increasing the individual's level of stress, anxiety and anguish.

O balance is fundamental for general motor coordination, because poor balance affects the construction of the body schema, as it results in the loss of awareness of certain parts of the body. For him, the more defective the balance, the more energy is expended, resulting in psychological consequences such as anxiety and insecurity (LOPES & FARJALLA, 2009).

Velasco (1994) states that "attention and concentration are not enough, it is necessary to have an emotional, affective and bodily structure for static and dynamic balance".

"Balance is responsible for the position and distribution of weight in relation to space, time and the axis of gravity, and is therefore the basis of all global dynamic coordination." (BUENO, 1998).

For Rosa Neto (2002), body schema is the organization of sensations related to one's own body in association with data from the outside world, and in piano education it is the key to the whole organization of the personality.

According to Moraes (2004) apud Lopes & Farjalla (2009) body schema refers to the ability to accurately discriminate between body parts and the ability to organize body parts when performing a task. O which is understood como the unconscious image that a human being has of their body.

Alves (2003) apud Lopes & Farjalla (2009) says that spatial organization is an aspect of children's motor development, and is the basis for future discoveries of mathematical and written reading skills. Thus, the way the school environment is arranged is very important for spatial development and suggests that students take part in this arrangement, as this can encourage the development of their own spatial organization.

For Rosa Neto (2002), the evolution of spatial notation highlights the existence of two stages: one linked to the immediate perception of the environment, characterized by the perceptive or sensorimotor sphere; the other based on mental operations that emerge from the representative and intellectual sphere. This evolution follows that of the establishment of objective relationships in which the child, dominated at first by his egocentrism, gradually decentralizes to examine relationships from a different point of view.

Anyone who is unable to identify the dimensional space that surrounds them will not be able to locate themselves or settle in that same space (BUENO, 1998).

According to Rosa Neto (2002), awareness of time is structured around perceived changes - regardless of whether they are successive or long-lasting. Their retention is linked to memory and the codification of information contained in events. The aspects related to the perception of time evolve and mature with age.

According to Gallardo (2004) apud Lopes & Farjalla (2009), temporal organization is associated with the organs of hearing that work with vision and proprioceptive sensations. It consists of orienting oneself in time, situating the present in relation to before and after, and distinguishing slow from moderate and fast and the ability to follow different rhythms.

Rosa Neto (2002) also points out two major components of temporal organization: order, which would be the succession that exists between events that produce an irreversible physical order, and duration, which is the rhythm that brings together, that is, separates, two times: the beginning and the end.

According to Capon (1989), laterality is the knowledge of the difference between right and left, and the ability to control both sides of the body, together or separately, where unilateral movements involve the use of one side of the body, bilateral movements involve the use of both sides of the body and cross laterality is the simultaneous use of different limbs on opposite sides of the body.

Laterality, according to Rosa Neto (2002), is a function of a predominance that gives one of the two hemispheres the initiative in organizing the motor act, which will lead to learning and the consolidation of practices. This functional attitude, which supports intentionality, develops in a fundamental way at the moment of the investigative activity during which the child encounters his environment. The fundamental educational action to put the child in the best position to develop a defined laterality, respecting genetic and environmental factors, is the one that allows them to organize their motor activities.

4. THE STAGES OF MOTOR DEVELOPMENT ACCORDING TO PIAGET, VIGOTSKY AND WALLON

It is very important to highlight the contribution of Piaget, Wallen and Vygotsky to the stages of psychomotor development.

According to Oliveira (2001), the theories of Jean Piaget and Henri Wallen are the most complete and articulated genetic theories of psychological development. Unlike these two scholars, Vygotsky did not formulate a structured conception of human development, but he does offer us reflections and research data on various aspects of human development. In this way, Vygotsky (1978) reports that psychological development is structured on the basis of the social relationships established between the individual and the outside world.

Vygotsky (1978) states that the language that comes from play can be understood clearly and objectively and also represents a very important factor for the child's social, interpersonal, inter-relational and inter-family development, so that assimilation during lessons becomes easier.

According to Vygotsky (1989, p. 101), "human beings grow up in a social environment and interaction with other people is essential to their development". In fact, learning and development are interrelated from the moment a child comes into contact with the world.

The author goes on to say that in interaction with the social and physical environment, children develop in a more comprehensive and efficient way. This means that involvement with their social environment triggers various internal developmental processes that will allow them to reach a new level of development. In this way, the individual needs to interact with people in order to be a social being.

Thus, in the conception that it is learning that makes it possible to awaken the individual's internal processes, linking the person's development to their relationship with the sociocultural environment. Vygotsky (1984) postulates that there are two levels of actual and potential development.

According to Vygotsky (1984), the zone of proximal development refers to the path that the individual will take to develop functions that are in the process of maturing and which will become consolidated functions, established at their level of real development. The zone of proximal development is therefore a psychological domain in constant transformation: What a child can do with someone's help today, they will be able to do on their own tomorrow.

It's as if the process of development progressed more slowly than the process of learning; learning awakens processes of development which gradually become part of the individual's consolidated psychological functions. By constantly interfering in the child's zone of proximal development, adults and more experienced children help to move along the developmental processes of the immature members of the culture (VYGOTSKY, 1984).

The same author also states that learning and development are interrelated from the moment a child comes into contact with tho world. In interacting with the social and physical environment, the child develops in a more comprehensive and efficient way. This means that involvement with their social environment triggers various internal developmental processes that will allow them to reach a new level of development.

Vygotsky (1989) states that through observation, imitation and experimentation with instructions received from more experienced people, children experience various physical and cultural experiences, thus building up knowledge about tho world around them.

For Piaget (1979), the child's actions don't develop on the same piano in the sense that they become cumulative experiences; the child assimilates the world, builds cognitive schemes, reconstructs his experiences and at the same time builds his intelligence.

Piaget (1979) deals with the motor phases of children from birth. A baby feels its environment as part of itself. As it grows, and its nervous system matures, it expands its experiences and gradually begins to differentiate itself from its environment. It then comes to represent the elements of space, discovering shapes and dimensions and, with this, it begins to perfect and refine its movements, acquiring greater coordination within a given space and time. O development will follow certain periods: sensorimotor, pre-operational, concrete operational and formal operational, which Piaget (1979) describes as follows:

- Sensorimotor phase, from birth to approximately 2 years old, the period of reflexes, the child plays alone, without the use of rules.
- Pre-operational stage, from approximately 2 to 5 or 6 years old, the child is building up the ability to carry out logico-mathematical operations, acquires an awareness of the existence of rules and begins to play make-believe games with other children.
- Stage of concrete operations, from approximately 7 to 11 years of age, marked by the beginning of cooperation and logical

reasoning.

- The formal operant phase, from the age of 12 onwards, is the development of intelligence itself, which brings the individual into the world of formal operations.

According to Piaget (1979), play is a time when children are stimulated to represent their reality, their universe and independent selves. For example, they do not establish a realistic relationship with the objects around them, manipulating them in an individualized way. In other words, in play, children will be improving their ability to learn through the formulation of analogies, where they will develop personal characteristics to become an autonomous, critical, responsible and supportive person, thus creating their best adaptation to the world.

Wallon (1975) states that thought arises from the action and returns to it, the person is seen as a whole, including aspects of affectivity, motor skills and intelligence. For him, the development of intelligence depends on the experiences offered by the environment and the degree to which the subject makes use of them, whether in a discontinuous way or marked by ruptures and processes.

Mian (2003) reports that it is through play that children become intermediaries between internal and external reality, participating, understanding and perceiving themselves as an integral member of their social environment. It is also through playing that children stop being passive and become responsible for their actions, deciding the course of the socio-cultural situations they create and experience different feelings, which contributes to the formation of their personality.

Wallon (1975) apud Oliveira (2002) points out that every person constitutes a specific and optimal system of exchanges with the environment. This system integrates its actions in a process of functional equilibrium involving motor skills, affect and cognition, but in which, at each stage of development, one particular form of action predominates over the others.

In this way, Wallon (1975) classifies children into the following stages:

- Impulsive-emotional (1ª year of life) emotional relationships with the environment predominate in children.
- ªThe Sensorimotor Stage (1 to 3 years) is an intense exploration of the physical world in which cognitive relationships with the environment predominate.
- Personalism (3 to 6 years)the construction of self-consciousness

occurs through social relationships, directing the child's interest towards people, thus predominating affective relationships.

- Categorical Stage (6 years old) o interest is focused on knowledge and conquest of the outside world.

Thus, as the development of the individual is divided and classified into periods, motor skills have their own classifications and definitions.

5. MOTOR DEVELOPMENT AND LEARNING

Among the main reasons for the increased interest in knowledge about motor development are the parallels between motor development and cognitive development. There is a close relationship between what children are able to learn and what they are able to do. It is during childhood that a variety of forms of movement should be provided to ensure the child's proper development and growth, making them competent to respond to their needs and those of their environment (MIRANDA, RESEGUE, FIGUEIRAS, 2003). Therefore, child development and learning are related to motor skills and are of fundamental importance to the child's overall development (ROSA NETO, 2002).

According to Gallahue and Ozmun (2005), motor development is a sequential process, related to chronological age, brought about by the interaction between task requirements, the individual's biology and environmental conditions, and is inherent to social, intellectual and emotional changes.

The motor experience provides ample development of the different components of motor skills, such as coordination, balance and body schema. This development is fundamental, particularly in childhood, for the development of the various basic motor skills - walking, running, jumping, galloping, throwing and rebounding. It is during the childhood period, when the schooling process begins, that there is a large increase in motor skills, which enables children to master their bodies in different activities (Gallahue and Ozmun, 2005).

Rosa Neto (2002) also points out that motor activity is of the utmost importance for children's overall development and that it is through motor exploration that children develop an awareness of themselves and the outside world. In this way, the acquisition of motor skills is integrally linked to the development of the perception of body, space and time. These skills constitute basic mastery components for both motor learning and school education activities.

According to Souza Neto (2002), exploring movements and increasing their motor repertoire are factors that favor the motor, cognitive, social and affective development that children need. In this sense, everyday life is also important for the learning process in the formation of the subject and in the construction of history. According to the same author, children need to adapt to the environment and the method by which learning takes place, so that they can consolidate the assimilation and application of concepts to the process of building their social and cultural relationships.

As Souza Neto (2002) points out, learning goes beyond literacy, but literacy is important for ensuring that the subject has the personal tools to decipher the codes and signs required in the process of learning to read and write.

On the other hand, many children find it difficult to carry out motor activities, which can have a negative impact on their performance at school. According to Baltazar (2001), most children with learning difficulties in reading and writing have the same way of relating to the other areas worked on in school. The problems related to school retention are evident and, although the importance of these problems is recognized, the identification of children with learning difficulties at school is growing (OKANO et al., 2004).

Piaget (1979) believes that human development is subordinated to two groups of factors: hereditary factors and biological adaptation (maturation of certain nervous tissues, increase in the size and complexity of the Central Nervous System, growth of bones and muscles) and environmental factors (experience and sensorimotor stimulation, nutrition, socio-economic and affective conditions). In other words, stimulating children from an early age is fundamental. Their basic needs should be met as much as possible during this period. Children who lack bodily and environmental stimulation at this stage may present difficulties during other stages of development, with the risk of arriving at school with accumulated deficits in relation to the minimum skills necessary for them to acquire new behaviors that will be required of them (LAMPREIA, 1985).

Lampreia (1985) also states that the delay in the psychomotor development of disadvantaged children can largely be attributed to the fact that they grew up in an environment lacking in stimuli to facilitate it.

6. ROSA NETO'S MOTOR DEVELOPMENT SCALE

The Motor Development Scale (MDS) is an instrument developed by Rosa Neto (2002) with the aim of carrying out a psychomotor assessment of children. It includes a set of highly diversified tests of graduated difficulty with the aim of measuring children's motor development. This instrument can be used to detect characteristics of children's development, whether there are delays in motor development and disturbances in balance, coordination, laterality, agility, sensitivity, body schema, spatial structure and orientation, graphism, affectivity, etc. (Santos, 2006).

The human organism has a biological logic, an organization, a maturing and evolutionary calendar, a door open to interaction and stimulation. Between birth and adulthood, profound changes take place. Children's motor skills evolve greatly with age and become increasingly varied, complete and complex (ROSA NETO, 2002).

Rosa Neto (2002) states that there are countless tests for assessing children's motor development, however, almost none of these instruments manage to fully encompass all aspects of development. One of these that tends to contribute to a complete and elucidating assessment of motor development is the scale, which has a method of applying tests that are attractive to the child and comprises a set of diversified tests of graduated difficulty, covering different areas of motor development.

The Motor Development Scale (MDS), developed by Francisco Rosa Neto (2002), was used to develop this study.

EDM works as an indispensable complement to a correct diagnosis and is a fundamental element for the professional who uses it to intervene in the most appropriate way for the individual's pattern, based on the results obtained.

According to Rosa Neto (2002), it assesses the level of motor development through 51 tests covering the specific areas of fine motor skills, global motor skills, balance, body schema, spatial and temporal organization and laterality. The scale considers successes and failures, taking into account the standards established by the author. It is an individual assessment mechanism suitable for children aged between 2 and 11 who have difficulties in learning at school, delays in neuropsychomotor development, problems with speech, writing and calculation, conduct problems (hyperactivity, anxiety, lack of motivation, etc.), neurological, mental and sensory alterations, etc.

According to Rosa Neto (2002), the participants are assessed on the basis of the test corresponding to 1 year prior to their current chronological age on the day of the test in each motor skill, and the assessment is only interrupted when they have not succeeded in the proposed task. This final result is called the motor age, which corresponds to that motor skill, and when compared to the chronological age, we determine the classification of motor progress or delay. In the appendices is table 1.0, which shows the tasks in Rosa Neto's test (2002).

The results are recorded on the answer sheet. According to Rosa Neto (2002), the symbol "1" is used when the individual succeeds in the test, "1/2" if the test has a positive result with only one limb and "0" if the result is negative, where the individual's motor age is determined by the last test in which he/she succeeded.

For the test, according to Rosa Neto (2002), the following materials are needed: six 2.5cm cubes; thread n^0 60; sewing needle (1cm x 1mm); a 45cm shoe string; sexagesimal stopwatch; tissue paper; rubber ball or court tennis ball - 6cm in diameter; white cardboard; pencil n^0 2; eraser; blank sheets of paper; 15cm high stool; 2m rope; elastic band; jumping stand; a box of matches; a 45cm high chair; a tray with 3 geometric shapes; 5 and 6 cm long sticks; a rectangle; two cardboard triangles; 3 cubes of different colors;

figures of a schematic doll; a ball; scissors; a 15cm x 25cm card with a 0.5cm hole in the center; a cardboard tube and complementary sheets.

According to Rosa Neto (2002), each motor age is associated with an index called the Motor Quotient, calculated from the ratio between motor age and chronological age. This index indicates how far along the child is in the development of that skill. Table 2 below shows the classification of the individual based on the Motor Quotient.

Class Range	**Classification**
130 or more	Much lower
120-129	Superior
110-119	Normal High
90-109	Normal Medium
80-89	Normal Low
70-79	Bottom
69 or less	Much lower

Source: Rosa Neto (2002)

In addition, according to Rosa Neto (2002), the general development of the individual is interpreted through an index called the Global Motor

Quotient found by calculating the arithmetic mean of the Motor Quotients of all the Skills.

Thus, the EDM is an important ally in measuring children's motor development so that the intervention of the Physical Education professional can be meaningful in terms of promoting improvements in children's motor development.

7. METHODOLOGY

This research is characterized as indirect and its design is bibliographic. According to Gil (2002, p. 59):

Bibliographical research, like any other type of research, takes place over a series of stages. Their number, as well as their sequence, depends on many factors, such as the nature of the problem, the level of knowledge that the researcher has on the subject, the degree of precision that the research is intended to provide, etc.

According to what has been written, the factors influencing this research already give an indication of its design, as mentioned above.

"In bibliographical research for a monograph, dissertation or thesis, the researcher is not simply a reader of books and magazines in the library. He is a determined operator in search of sources." (BOAVENTURA, 2004, p. 69).

Therefore, this work is not just about finding sources and putting the authors' ideas 'loose' on the pages. The search for materials follows the purpose of answering the problem raised in the introduction in order to achieve the established objective.

7.1 BIBLIOGRAPHIC SURVEY

In order to answer the problem and achieve the objective of this work through bibliographical research, it was first necessary to carry out a bibliographical survey.

Andrade (2003, p. 87) states that: "Once you have a list of bibliographical indications on the subject you want to focus on, you proceed to survey the works that will be read and annotated."

According to Gil (2002), this bibliographical survey can be understood as an exploratory study, since its purpose is to provide familiarity with the area of study to be approached.

Therefore, the materials that were of the utmost importance for data collection came from common reading books, dictionaries and encyclopedias, scientific articles and scientific journals.

7.2 OBTAINING THE MATERIAL

All the material collected and used in this work was obtained from libraries or via the internet. The library of the Federal Institute of Piaui (IFPI), Floriano Campus, was the most used for borrowing books for current reading. The internet was a great source for dictionaries and encyclopedias, scientific articles, scientific journals, master's dissertations and government documents.

Many of the sources come from electronic media, as they are very up-to-date and easily accessible. However, only reliable sources have been included in the work (those already known in the academic world, with the indication of authors and other necessary requirements according to each work mentioned).

7.3 READING THE MATERIAL

The material was read as suggested by Andrade (2003): starting with a preliminary reading (or pre-reading), then a selective reading and then a critical (or reflective) reading. Pre-reading will make it possible to select the works that will be used for selective reading. Selective reading will locate the works or chapters or parts that contain useful information for the work in question. Critical or reflective reading allows the fundamental ideas of each text to be grasped (ANDRADE, 2003, p. 87).

7.4 SUMMARIZING THE MATERIAL

After reading the aforementioned material, reading sheets were made up. These were bibliographic sheets, i.e. to write down the bibliographic references to be used in the work. These reading sheets contained the identification of works and contents, analysis of texts, citations and, finally, interpretations that provided a theoretical basis for the research described here (GIL, 2002).

7.5 CONTENT ANALYSIS

After an in-depth study of the selected material, the bibliographical review was written, which preceded the analysis and discussion of the data. At this point, three basic themes were established for discussion: the relationship between motor development and psychomotricity, the importance of motor development in the learning process and the importance of Rosa Neto's motor development scale in the study and research of psychomotricity.

8. CONTENT ANALYSIS AND DISCUSSION

In view of what has been studied and presented in the theoretical framework of this work, the relationship between motor development and psychomotricity is understood to be close, given that motor development is the field of research that studies motor behavior (standard skills, motor generalizations and physical abilities) and the theories that underpin the significance of human movement in the process of human development and learning. Psychomotricity is the science that studies man through his body in movement and in relation to his internal and external world, and is related to the maturation process, where the body is the origin of cognitive, affective and organic acquisitions.

Based on this context, we realize that psychomotricity needs to be seen in a positive light by education professionals, as it helps the student's motor and intellectual development, with the body and mind being integrated elements of their formation.

It is important to understand the importance of development in the teaching-learning process of children, taking into account the applicability of this knowledge in the assessment of children's development and in the analysis of motor skills. Throughout our study, we realized that all the authors studied consider that motor development plays a major role in cognitive learning, i.e. the child's development is closely linked to experience. In other words, it is through action that children learn and discover themselves.

In short, it can be said that learning results from perspective mechanisms in their dialectical relationship with motor mechanisms, and that it is through movement that the human being learns bio-psycho-socially.

In this sense, it is also important to point out that Rosa Neto's Motor Development Scale is of great importance when it comes to ascertaining potentials for developing certain skills, because through these actions, potentials for developing certain skills can be found in children.

From this perspective, Rosa Neto (2002) has made a major contribution to motor development studies, because with the creation of his scale, an instrument capable of measuring the development of motor skills emerged in the scientific universe. For the scientific community, this instrument conveys a high degree of reliability for the analysis of motor development, while it is a highly accessible and easy-to-use mechanism for carrying out tests, which makes it possible to investigate this process to a greater extent.

9. FINAL CONSIDERATIONS

The aim of this research was to answer the following questions: What is the importance of the rosa neto motor development scale as a tool for assessing children's motor development?

The initial hypothesis is that the Motor Development Scale is a great tool for investigating the development of motor skills in children and young people.

The research has shown that the Motor Development Scale is of great importance in ascertaining potential to develop certain skills, as well as contributing to motor development studies, because with the creation of this scale, a reliable and easy-to-use instrument has emerged in the scientific community, capable and insightful for measuring the development of motor skills.

In conclusion, research is needed both to corroborate the facts and conclusions presented here and to challenge and disagree with the concepts put forward. We also believe that it is important for field research to emerge, based on the credibility of the rosa neto motor development scale, in order to ascertain the levels of motor development of children attending the initial and final grades of elementary school in public and private schools, in order to quantify and characterize possible differences between stages of motor development, possible delays and, with the intention of making comparisons between the motor development of children in our municipality and others in our state and country.

REFERENCES

ANDRADE, Maria Margarida de. **Introdugao a metodologia do trabalho cientifico:** elaboração de **trabalhos** na graduação. 6. ed. Sao Paulo: Atlas, 2003. 174 p.

BALTAZAR, M. O treatment of learning difficulties in reading and writing in the light of constructivist psychopedagogy. **Revista Reflexao e Agao**, Santa Cruz do Sul, v. 9, n. 1, p. 37-46, 2001.

BOAVENTURA, Edivaldo M. **Metodologia da pesquisa:** monografia, dissertaçãoo, tese. Sao Paulo: Atlas, 2004. 160 p.

BUENO, J. M. **Psicomotricidade teorica e pratica:** Stimulación, Educación e reeducación psicomotora com atividades aquaticas. Sao Paulo: Lovise, 1998.

CAPON. **Classroom pianos for perceptual-motor activities.** Novo Hamburgo, RS: Feevale: Manole, 1989.

FONSECA, Vitor da. *Psychomotor development and learning.* Porto Alegre: Artmed, 2008.

FONSECA, Vitor **da.Manual de observação psicomotora:** significação psiconeurologica dos fatores psicomotores. Porto Alegre: Artes Medicas,

1995.

GALLARDO, P. S. Jorge; **Physical Education, Contributions to professional training.** 4. ed. Ijui: Unijui, 2004.

Gallahue DL, Ozmun JC. **Understanding motor development:** babies, children, adolescents and adults. Sao Paulo: Ed. Phorte; 2005.

GIL, Antonio Carlos. **How to prepare research projects.** 4. ed. Sao Paulo: Atlas, 2002.175 p.

LAMPREIA, C. (1985). Prevention in developmental delay: prevention in psychology. *Ciencia e Profissao,5,* (1) p. 25-30.

LEVIN, Esteban. The psychomotor clinic: the body in language. Petropolis: Vozes, 2000.

LIMA, A.S; BARBOSA, S.B. **Psicomotricidade na educagao infantil.** Sao Joao de Meriti:October, 2011.

LOPES, Gabriela Beghini; FARJALLA, Renato, **motor development of preschool children from public and private schools in petropolis. R.** Mln. Educ. Fls., Vigosa, v. 17, n. 1, p. 38-49, 2009.

MIAN, R. **Monitor ou recreação:** Formação profissional. Sao Paulo: Texto novo, 2003.

MIRANDA, L.P; RESEGUE, R; FIGUEIRAS, A.C.M. A criança e o

adolescente com problemas do desenvolvimento no ambulatorio de pediatria. **Jornal de Pediatria**, Rio de Janeiro, v.79, n.1, 2003.

NUNEZ, J. A.G; BERRUEZZO, P. P. **Psychomotricity and Early Childhood Education,** Sciences of pre-school and special education. Madrid, 1994.

OKANO, C. B.; LOUREIRO, S. R.; LINHARES, M. B. M.; MARTURANO, E. M. Children with school difficulties assisted in a psycho-pedagogical support program: evaluation of self-concept. **Psicologia: reflexao e cntica**, Porto Alegre, v. 17, n. 1, p.121-128, 2004.

OLIVEIRA, G.C. **Psicomotricidade:** Educagao e Reeducagao num enfoque Psicopedagogico. 5. ed. Rio de Janeiro: Vozes, 2001.

OLIVEIRA, Z.de M. R. de. **Early childhood education:** foundations and methods.
Sao Paulo: Cortez, 2002.

PEREZ, Raquel Augusto dos Santos; BOECK, Ursula; CAMPOS Miriam Piber. **The symbology of movement,** psychomotricity and education... Sao Paulo: Lovise, 2000.

PIAGET, Jean. **Learning and Knowledge.** Rio de Janeiro: Freitas Bastos, 1979.

ROSA NETO, Francisco; et all. **The importance of motor assessment in schoolchildren: analysis of the reliability of the Motor Development Scale,** 2010.

ROSA NETO, Francisco. **Manual of motor assessment.** Porto Alegre: Artmed Editora, 2002.

SANTOS, R. P. *Psicomotricidade.* Sao Paulo: Course Pack, 2006.

SANTOS, S.; DANTAS, L.; OLIVEIRA, J. A. **Motor development in children, the elderly and people with coordination disorders.** Revista paulista de educagao fisica V. 18, aug. 2004, p. 33-44.

SILVA, D.; FALKENBACH, A. Psychomotricity: a descriptive look at its different aspects. Available at <http://www.rededapsicomotricidade.com .br/linkart.html> Accessed: March 25, 2013.

BRAZILIAN SOCIETY OF PSYCHOMOTRICITY. Available at: HTTP://www.psicomotricidade.com.br/apsicomotricidade.htm.Acessoem: 12/01/2013.

SOUZA, Samanta Garcia de; URZEDA, Wesley; SOUZA, Sabrina Garcia de. **Motor development scale: evaluation and expansion of motor skills using sports content: a review.** EFDeportes.com, Digital Magazinc. Buenos Aires, 2011.

SOUZA NETO,J.C.A aprendizagem na formacao do sujeito. **Notebooks de Psicopedagogia**, Sao Paulo, v.1, n. 2, p. 12-27, 2002.

VELASCO, C. G. **Psychomotor skills and rehabilitation in water.** Sao Paulo: Harbra, 1994.

VYGOTSKY, L. **The social formation of the mind.** Sao Paulo: Martins Fontes,

1984

VYGOTSKY, L. S. **The social formation of the mind.** Sao Paulo: Martins Fontes, 1989.

VYGOTSKY, L. S. **Pensamento e linguagem.** Rio de Janeiro: Martins Fontes, 1978.

WALLON, H. **Psicologiae educagao da infancia.** Lisbon: Estampa, 1975.

MIX
Papier aus verantwortungsvollen Quellen
Paper from responsible sources
FSC® C105338

Printed by Books on Demand GmbH, Norderstedt / Germany